D0348070

lean for
practitioners

*An introduction to Lean
for healthcare organisations*

MARK EATON

Lean for Practitioners
© Mark Eaton

Book Typesetting by Neil Coe
neil@cartadesign.co.uk
Set in Delicious 10 on 15pt

First published in 2008 by;
Ecademy Press
6 Woodland Rise, Penryn,
Cornwall UK TR10 8QD
info@ecademy-press.com
www.ecademy-press.com

Printed and Bound by;
Lightning Source in the UK and USA

Printed on acid-free paper from managed forests. This book is printed on demand, so no copies will be remaindered or pulped.

ISBN 978-1-905823-39-0

Author's Introduction

The concept for this book came about when I found myself being told by more and more people that they understood the 'tools' of Lean but not how you converted them into improvements, fundamentally asking 'How do you actually 'become' Lean?'

In writing this book I set out to create a practical introduction to the key aspects of Lean with the minimum of fuss and jargon and that tries to help you plan the first steps on your journey to Lean. I have deliberately not tried to paraphrase the many excellent books that go into the detail of the tools of Lean (although I have introduced you to some of the key ones to help steer your further reading), but have focused on the concepts and process of 'Lean' and in the journey, I hope I have created a useful introduction to 'going Lean'.

In terms of what qualifies me to write this book, I cut my 'Lean Teeth' in manufacturing before moving into consultancy where I got involved in setting up and running a wide range of publicly funded Lean programmes for various public bodies, including the DTi and various Regional Development Agencies. Subsequently, on my journey I worked with the armed forces and the wider public sector before I found my passion working with the Healthcare Sector.

I need to state that whilst I am a big fan of using an approach based on Lean to improve healthcare processes, I am not a 'tool head' or a 'Lean Freak' who believes that it is only Lean can transform Healthcare and recognise that sometimes other approaches (for example Theory of Constraints or Six Sigma) might better fit particular scenarios and there is a need for organisations to be flexible in their approach, choosing the best and most appropriate set of tools for the issues they are tackling.

Beyond helping people to understand the practicalities of 'going Lean', my real interest is in how to convert simple changes into long-term improvements and that is the subject of our book Sustaining Lean Healthcare Programmes written by my friend and colleague Simon Phillips and myself. The concepts in each book are designed to 'link together' with the minimum of duplication, extra (wasted) words or unnecessary detail.

I see this book evolving over time based on your feedback and a process of continuous improvement that all of us need to be on if we are truly to become Lean. Email me your thoughts and ideas for improvement to markeaton@amnis-uk.com.

Contents

Chapter 1

So, what is this thing called Lean?

At its heart, Lean is simply a philosophy designed to help organisations identify the activities that are preventing them from being effective and eliminate them using a systematic approach and a range of improvement tools. I tend to refer to Lean simply as 'Structured Common Sense'.

As a concept, Lean is very easy to understand, which is both a blessing and a curse because whilst it is good that people can quickly understand the benefits it can take a long time to learn how to apply the tools properly, which is why so many 'Lean' programmes fail to deliver the improvements people thought they would or fail to embed themselves in the organisation. In addition, most people who 'do Lean' only ever learn one or two tools (usually 5S and Process Mapping) and because of this limited exposure to Lean they believe that this is the extent of it.

In reality Lean is a very deep concept that can be applied

strategically (to set the direction of the whole organisation or pathway for example) or tactically (to fix a single problem within a pathway, process or area).

Although some people think of Lean as a modern management fad, it actually evolved out of the Toyota Production System which was developed in the 1950's. The father of TPS (and the Grandfather of Lean) was Taiichi Ohno, a production engineer at Toyota, who first identified that much of what the company were doing was not adding any value to the end customer, and was therefore tying up resources wastefully – and he also developed or modified a range of tools[1] to enable the employees at Toyota to spot these wastes and make improvements. In addition, just to show how old the basis of Lean is, Taiichi Ohno is on record as saying that he drew some of his thinking from the work of Henry Ford at the turn of the 20th Century.

In the mid-90's, James Womack and Dan Jones first coined the phrase Lean[2] and it is their methodology that has been widely adopted, although in many ways Lean is the wrong name for what they proposed as to most people it means 'cutting to the bone' or 'devoid of excess fat' and therefore can appear very threatening.

A better name for what Lean is capable of providing to an organisation is 'Fit' (as it makes the organisation fit for purpose) or 'Flexible' (as it enables their processes to react quickly) – but Lean is the common name we now use and to avoid confusion I will stick with that name throughout this book.

1 The most common tools of Lean will be explained later, although we only touch on them in this text.
2 In the book 'Lean Thinking' (Womack & Jones)

The most important thing to remember about Lean is that your team is generally doing the best they can with problematic processes and that it is the processes that are faulty, not the people!

So, why do processes break down? It is not as if someone sits down with a piece of paper when they are planning a new process and 'designs in' complexity and the need for extra effort is it? Of course not! What really happens is that people design processes to tackle a specific set of issues and sometimes they forget the upstream and downstream effects of what they have designed (which is why you should always look at a process 'End to End' (E2E)) but more often the effect of time changes the parameters of the process, something I have shown pictorially below:

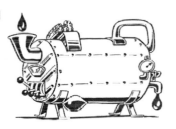

When the process is first designed it is like an 'efficient machine' where the energy in equals the energy out and there are only a few 'losses'. The process works efficiently and the machine does not breakdown very often.

However, sometimes very quickly, sometimes more slowly, the effect of time will cause the process to degrade and the machine will start to breakdown, leak and generally become inefficient.

Many people in Healthcare say that they feel that they are working harder today than they used to and the function of Lean is to 'reset' the machine back to its original settings so that it is more efficient but recognising that the effects of time will cause the process to degrade again. This is why Lean is often described as a Journey rather than a single destination.

Your Top Points From This Chapter

-

-

-

-

-

Chapter 2

The Key Lean Concepts

At its heart, Lean sees the world in 'Black & White' (well, Red & Green really). Red indicates activities that are 'Non-Value Adding' (activities that tie up cost/time/resources but add 'No Value' to the customer) and Green indicates activities that do 'Add Value' (being activities the customer 'wants' and would be prepared to pay for if they had to). Lean therefore is simply a philosophy to enable organisations to 'see' Non Value Adding activity and then eliminate it.

In this chapter, we introduce the key concepts of Lean: Value Adding & Non-Value Adding Activities, The 7 Wastes (+1), The 5 Key Principles of Lean, The Hierarchy of Improvement and Designing a realistic 'Future State'

Value Adding (VA) & Non-Value Adding (NVA) Activities

As already mentioned, Lean sees the world as either **red** or **green**.

○ In the **green** corner we have activities which are seen as **'Value Adding' (VA)**. These are activities which are defined as something that the customer wants, is aware of and would be prepared to 'pay for' (if appropriate). In industry, Value Adding steps often 'transform' the product in some ways, whilst in a Healthcare context value adding activities increase the value of information in a process, improve the health of a patient or delivers an essential service.

○ In the **red** corner we have activities which are **Non Value Adding (NVA)** (otherwise referred too as 'Waste' or 'Muda' in other texts), which are things that the customer does not want or does not care about and for which they would not be prepared to 'pay for'.

In a typical process, Non-Value Adding (NVA) activities far outweigh the Value Adding (VA) ones with the typical spread of Value Adding Activities being 1-25% in a Healthcare environment, meaning that between 75% and 99% are Non-Value Adding (NVA).

This simple two colour approach to defining activities causes some people lots of problems as there is often confusion about things that have to be done but which the customer sees no value in at all. It is important to state that just because something has to be done does not make it automatically Value Adding!

For example, just because I have to go and collect swabs four times per shift from a storage facility does not make the activity value adding. Also, just because I have to file a 'call report' after each call (because it is in the procedures) does not make it automatically value adding either.

This is an essential concept as without it every activity will be seen as Value Adding, and the reality of Lean is that you **always attack the Non-Value Adding activity first** as this is the bit that customers don't want and don't care about but which is adding unnecessary costs and time to the process.

There are categories of Non-Value Adding (such as Tests or Inspections) that you may never eliminate or may not want to eliminate but which are fundamentally NOT Value Adding. These could be termed **'Essential Non-Value Adding'** activities but using that term implies that in addition to the **red** and **green** colours of Lean we might want to have an **amber/yellow** colour.

I am completely against this – even if something is Essential Non-Value Adding it should still be **red.** The reason for this being that as soon as it goes **yellow** it will be treated just the same as **green** (Value Adding) and the team will stop focusing on improving it!

To help with assessing whether an activity is Value Adding or not, there is a useful concept called **VotC** (Voice of the Customer) that basically requires you to speak to your customer (who in Healthcare are predominantly, but not exclusively, patients) and put yourself in their shoes and then designing your processes and services to deliver what your customers view as 'Value Adding'.

To categorise items as 'Value Adding' they should pass the following test:

1. Does the customer value the service/activity

2. Does the customer 'experience' the service/activity (are they aware of it)

3. Is it **impossible** to remove or change the service/activity without the customer noticing

If the answer is 'Yes' to all three of the above, the activity can be classed as Value Adding. If the answer is no to any of them, then the item is likely to be 'Non Value Adding'.

It is a fact that you will spend a long time discussing which activities are Value Adding and which are Non-Value Adding and this should be viewed as a healthy and helpful debate!

The 7 Wastes (+1) (aka Waste or Muda)

When he was developing the Toyota Production System, Taiichi Ohno spent time trying to categorise the types of Non-Value Adding activity that was present within the process. This was finally coded into the '7 Wastes' (or Seven Deadly Sins).

Two of the original wastes (Motion & Transport) are closely related, with 'Motion' being the movement of human beings (such as walking back and forth to a sluice room) and 'Transport' being the movement of things (such as transporting drugs from one site to another. Most people now recognise an 8th Waste (or 7 Wastes + 1) this being the waste of Talent, being the inappropriate use of people's skills.

By grouping Motion & Transport together and adding in Talent we can organise the 7 Wastes (+1) into the acronym 'WORMPIT':

- Waiting
- Over-Processing (aka Over Production)
- Rework (aka Correction)
- Motion (& Transportation)
- Processing Waste
- Inventory
- Talent

The definitions of these seven 'WORMPIT' categories of Non-Value Adding activities (or Waste/Muda) are shown below:

- **Waiting** – time when customers (or their information, services or products) are held up or when the customer is waiting for activity to commence

- **Over-Processing** – doing more activity than is required or producing more outputs than are required

- **Rework** – (aka Correction) this is concerned with correcting mistakes or having to re-do work incorrectly done by someone else

- **Motion (& Transport)** – this is the waste of people and things having to move whilst undertaking activities

- **Processing Waste** – these are things that just don't need to be done (ie unnecessary tasks)

- ○ **Inventory** – stacking or queuing customers, information or materials

- ○ **Talent** – the waste of misusing people's skills and destroying their enthusiasm

The 5 Lean Principles

In the original book 'Lean Thinking' (which was focused on manufacturing) the authors identified 5 'Key Principles of Lean Systems and Organisations'. Given that Lean in a Healthcare context requires a different approach (mostly because patients are not quite like products and also pathways interact in a different way to production lines and have a different risk profile), I have modified the wording of the original 5 Principles to recognise these differences.

The 5 Principles are shown in the figure below and described in more detail underneath.

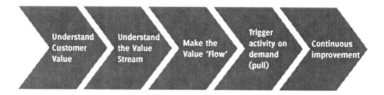

1st Principle: Understand Customer Value

The first principle is concerned with listening to the 'Voice of the Customer' (VotC) and determining what the customer perceives as 'Value Adding'. In a Healthcare context, patients are normally the primary customer but there could be others who are important. One recommendation is to identify who your 'prime' customers are (no more than 3) and then to work out what each customer group sees as value adding.

2nd Principle: Understand the Value Stream[3]

Having identified what your customers view as 'Value Adding' you must then understand how you deliver this value by analysing the steps in the 'Value Stream' that converts inputs to outputs (such as converting unwell patients into healthy patients).

We cover more about this process later in the book when we talk about Value Stream Analysis Events (VSE).

3rd Principle: Make the 'Value' Flow

Having understood how you deliver value (ie the Value Stream), the next principle is to make the value 'flow' by eliminating bottlenecks, bringing value adding steps closer together (both in terms of physical distance and in terms of the time between steps), eliminating 'batching' (stacking activities and doing them all at once) and moving towards a 'Continuous Flow' process.

I have shown below a process that flows based on a local 'hand car washing' facility near to where I live. The basic process takes 6 minutes and consists of three stages; Wash the Car, Wax/Shampoo and Rub In/Dry. Each step takes 2 minutes and the tools/equipment required for each step is located in the right place. Through this process the team can 'clean' 30 cars per hour.

3 'Pathway' is the commonly used Healthcare term that means the same as Value Stream

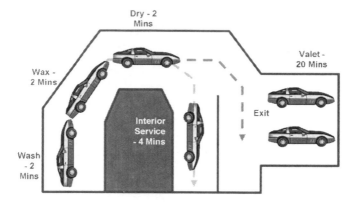

For the majority of cars, they will then drive straight out, but for a minority they will also have an interior service (vacuum and window clean) that lasts four minutes and they have designed the process so that the minority (about 10% of people) who want an interior service does not stop the main 'flow' of customers. Lastly, on a very few occasions, customers will want a 'valet' that lasts 20 minutes and they have the ability to remove the cars from the process to deal with these unusual activities.

In Lean terminology, it is common to talk about Runners, Repeaters and Strangers, with Runners being the 'common' activities, Repeaters being less common but still regular and Strangers being 'odd ball' activities. In the example given, the basic 6 minute wash is the 'Runner', the 4 minute interior valet is the 'Repeater' and the 20 minute valet is a 'Stranger'.

In the example given, they have designed the process to cope with the most common activities (Runners & Repeaters) and have considered how to deal with the less common activities (Strangers) but have not got a dedicated team to deal with them in the way that they have for the Runners and Repeaters and this is the essence of a process 'flowing'.

4th Principle: Trigger Activity on Demand (Pull)

The fourth Lean Principle is concerned with not undertaking activity (or producing items) until there is a 'Pull' from the customer to do so. The idea of 'Pull' in a Healthcare context is to keep the process working by drawing resources/patients/ materials to the point at which they are needed to prevent the process stopping.

To illustrate this, I will use a recent example of a 'Pull' system that I saw operating in an Outpatients Clinic (specifically a Rheumatology Clinic). I have created a representation of the clinic in the figure below.

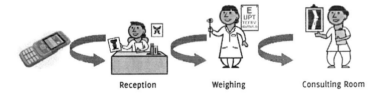

Reception   Weighing   Consulting Room

The aim of the 'Pull' was to keep the clinic 'flowing' and to maximise the consultant's utilisation. In this example, as one patient left the consulting room, the patient who had just been weighed is 'pulled' into see the consultant. This triggers another patient to be 'pulled' from the waiting area by reception so that they can be weighed and made ready to go into the consulting room next. Finally, 24 hours prior to the appointment, patients are 'pulled' via a text message to remind them to attend.

5th Principle: Continuous Improvement

The last principle is concerned with Continuous Improvement
in the process, looking again at the first four principles and
seeing what further improvements can be achieved, but also
dealing with changes in customer expectations, new policies
and procedures etc.

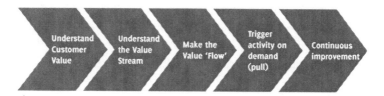

The Hierarchy of Improvement

The 'Hierarchy of Improvement' is a useful three stage thought
process that is used in Lean Projects to steer the improvement
process and is shown below:

- ○ Aim first to **Eliminate** the Non-Value Adding activity

- ○ if you can't eliminate it, can you **Reduce** the size (or
  impact) of the activity

- ○ if you can't reduce it, can you **Combine** it with another
  activity

When approaching improvements, the focus should always be
on eliminating Non-Value Adding (NVA) activities as it releases
the most resources (people, time, money etc) and often reduces
risk by the greatest percentage.

If you cannot completely eliminate the activity, then the next step is to look at the possibility of reducing it – for example reducing the amount of information required to be completed or reducing the distance travelled.

Lastly, if you cannot reduce it, the third step is to explore whether you can combine the activity with another one so that it becomes less of a burden on the organisation.

It is sometimes possible to combine the second and third steps – for example, first reducing an activity and then combining two activities together to get even more benefit!

Earlier in this chapter I mentioned the issue of 'Essential Non-Value Adding' activities. These are activities that are fundamentally Non-Value Adding but which you cannot or do not want to eliminate. The hierarchy of improvement (Eliminate, Reduce, Combine) allows you to look at Reducing or Combining these activities without having to 'Eliminate' them – and it is for this reason that I suggested you should never be tempted to use **amber/yellow** to describe Essential Non-Value Adding activities.

Designing a realistic 'Future State'

The last concept that I am going to cover in this chapter is the concept of designing a realistic 'Future State' for your Value Stream, this being an essential part of the 'Understanding the Value Stream' (as defined in the 5 Principles above). The 'Future State' defines how you will 'operate' an 'End to End' (E2E) Value Stream/Pathway or even an entire Organisation in the 'Future' (normally with the 'Future State' being set 6-18 Months ahead).

The design of a 'Future State' is a creative process which aims to change the way that people think about how they deliver services currently and enables participants to create a solution that is closest to being 'optimal' (in Lean terms this means being closest to eliminating all Non-Value Adding activities but also has the minimum patient safety risk exposure).

Designing a realistic 'Future State' is normally undertaken prior to the start of 'Rapid Improvement Events' and is created during a 'Value Stream Analysis Event'[4] . Without designing a realistic 'Future State', there is a danger of improving one part of a process in isolation and sub-optimising another part of the process by just transferring risk and costs elsewhere in the pathway.

The process of designing a 'Future State' via a 'Value Stream Analysis Event' consists of three steps and the key concept at each step is to look at the Pathway from End to End (E2E) to avoid isolated improvements and reduce the potential of simply transferring risks/issues elsewhere:

[4] Value Stream Mapping Events (VSE) are defined in more detail later in this document.

1. **Understand the Current State** – this is the process of working with a cross-functional team to understand how the process currently operates and where the issues/ risks are arising.

2. **Create a 'Blue Sky' Vision** – this creative process is designed to get the team thinking about a 'step change' in improvements (and avoids them getting locked into just tinkering with the 'Future State') and works by asking the team to design the 'Ideal' process based on a clean sheet of paper.

3. **Design a realistic 'Future State'** – once the Blue Sky vision has been created, it is important to identify the key concepts that you can take forward and use in a realistic 'Future State' with the aim of achieving a 30%+ improvement in performance across a range of measures/areas.

The three steps involved in designing a realistic 'Future State' are shown diagrammatically below. In Lean terms, the 'Future State' is often referred too as 'True North' – being the direction that the organisation should head toward.

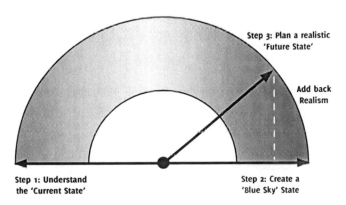

Step 3: Plan a realistic 'Future State'

Add back Realism

Step 1: Understand the 'Current State'

Step 2: Create a 'Blue Sky' State

More detail about the design of a realistic 'Future State' is given later in this book when we discuss the 'Value Stream Analysis Event' process.

Chapter 1 Key Concepts Summary

- **Value Adding (VA)** – Something that adds value to the customer is defined as something they are aware of and something they want. Typically only 1-25% of the activities in a pathway or process are Value Adding

- **Non-Value Adding (VA)** – Something that ties up resources/money/time and which is not something the customer wants and/or cares about. Typically, 75-99% of the time from the start to the end of a process will be taken up with Non-Value Adding activities

- **Waste/Muda** – Alternative names for things which are Non-Value Adding

- **Essential Non-Value Adding** – Activities that are fundamentally Non-Value Adding but which you may not be able to eliminate (or may not want too) but that are still candidates for being reduced or combined with other activities.

- **VotC (Voice of the Customer)** – (pronounced Voit-Ka) The process of understanding exactly what the customer of the process sees as 'Value Adding'

- **WORMPIT Wastes** – The acronym for the 7 Wastes (+1) of Non-Value Adding activities in the service sector.

○ **Eliminate, Reduce, Combine** – A hierarchy of how you should approach improvement of Non-Value Adding activities in a Lean system – first try to eliminate the activity, if you can't eliminate it then reduce it and if you can't reduce it can you combine it with another activity

○ **5 Principles of Lean** – These define the 5 Principles of a Lean process, which are: Specify Value, Understand the Value Stream, Make the Process Flow, Trigger Activity On Demand (Pull) and Continuous Improvement

○ **Design a realistic 'Future State'** – designed using a 'Value Stream Analysis Event' using the following three step process: Understand the Current State, Create a 'Blue Sky' vision and Design a realistic 'Future State'.

Your Top Points From This Chapter

○
....

○
....

○
....

○
....

○
....

Chapter 3

Step by Step Guide to 'Going Lean'

This chapter outlines the first steps involved in going Lean. Later steps are explored in more detail in the book 'Sustaining Lean Healthcare Programmes' (Phillips & Eaton) but to kick this chapter off we will explore why so many Lean programmes fail to deliver the expected results.

The 8 most commonly cited reasons[5] for Lean programmes failing to achieve their long-term potential are captured using the acronym CRITICAL™[6] as detailed below:

○ **Communications** – failing to engage in two way dialogue with staff

○ **Resources** – failing to allocate the correct resources and time to a programme

○ **Involvement** – not gaining the commitment from the team or not involving the right people

5 Adapted from various texts including Daft & Noe (2000), Oxtoby, McGuinness & Morgan (2002) and research undertaken by the author and seperate research by Copeland (2006-7

6 CRITICAL™ is a trademark of Amnis Ltd that is freely available for use on the basis that its source is acknowledged.

○ **Training** – carrying out too little or too much training prior to starting implementation

○ **Implementation** – problems with the planning and implementation process

○ **Compass** – failing to set out the direction and vision for the improvement process

○ **Achievement** – not moving from discussion into action quickly enough

○ **Leadership** – problems with the behaviour of leaders at all levels or leadership systems

More details about CRITICAL can be found in the book 'Sustaining Lean Healthcare Programmes' (Phillips & Eaton) and it has been introduced here to set the scene for why the structure we introduce for 'Going Lean' is the way it is, as introduced in the next sections.

Introducing PRISM™[7]

In this section I introduce you to the PRISM approach to going Lean. PRISM is a 'Step by Step' approach to Lean that tackles the CRITICAL™ issues detailed above and is shown diagrammatically below.

7 PRISM™ is a trademark of Amnis Ltd but is freely available on the basis that its source is acknowledged.

In this book we are only concerned with the first three steps of PRISM as these are the ones relevant to the introduction of Lean, with the remaining two steps of PRIM covered in more detail in the book 'Sustaining Lean Healthcare Programmes' (Phillips & Eaton) as they specifically relate to embedding Lean into a healthcare organisation.

PRISM Step 1: Prepare

Prior to any actual implementation activity it is essential that organisations prepare themselves effectively. PRISM recognises that there are four activities that might occur as part of a Prepare Phase, namely:

1. Scoping the Improvement Programme

2. Identifying & Developing Change Agents

3. Communicating with your Staff

4. Gathering relevant information about the processes to be improved

In this short section, I have provided some details about how to Scope an improvement programme and also provided some thoughts on the various development activities that will need to be undertaken to support the process of improvement.

Scoping Session

A Scoping Session is perhaps the most important Lean Event
you could undertake as it sets the scope of the Lean Activities
and develops a Compelling Need for the organisation to change
that can be easily communicated. A proposed agenda for a
Scoping Session is provided in the Appendix with the main
points being:

- **Compelling Need** – It is important to develop a statement
  that outlines why the organisation/area needs to change,
  what will happen and what the expected benefits will be.

- **Measures of Success** – Having set the Compelling Need, it
  is important to select the key measures that will be used
  to assess the success of the programme with (ideally) no
  more than 7 key measures.

- **In Scope** – Ensuring that the right people are involved,
  you should then be thinking about who is 'In Scope' for
  being involved/consulted as part of the improvement
  process and it is often a surprisingly long list of people
  who need to play a part in the overall success.

- **Fixed Points, Risks & Issues** – In the process of
  transforming one area you might not want certain things
  to change, or you may already have things going on that
  the team need to consider. You should also consider
  what risks might need to be mitigated and what other
  issues (such as new policies, changes in infrastructure
  etc) will affect the programme of improvement.

- **Key Roles** – Who will be the key people involved in

the process? I would recommend you think about four groups of people, namely:

- **Improvement Sponsor/s** – board level champions for the programme of improvement

- **Change Agents** – the internal facilitators who will coordinate activities/events and undertake training

- **Process Owners** – the senior manager responsible for each area/pathway to be improved

- **Team Leaders** – the people who will lead each Lean Event (see later)

○ **Timescales, Action & Communication** – This is concerned with detailing what the timescales are for the programme, what specifically will happen and how you will set up a two-way communication system with your improvement teams.

Developing your Team

All Healthcare organisations will need to consider a variety of development activities for different groups from the high intensity development required to train your 'Change Agents' through to simple awareness sessions for the broader team.

I recognise four main groups who will need some development support, namely:

▷ **Change Agents** – Highly experienced key staff who

act as a central resource and advisory team to local improvement events run by Practitioners. They will facilitate improvements, carry out training and awareness sessions for all other staff and will be the repository of best practice in the organisation.

▷ **Practitioners** – Key staff who have gained experience in a wide range of events but who have an operational role (ie they are not full time change agents) but who are expected to take on a leadership role (at any level) in an improvement process.

▷ **Users** – People who have participated in a few Lean events or might reasonably be expected to be involved in the next 4-8 months.

▷ **The Aware** – This is the title for 'everyone else' who has not participated in a Lean event. This group still need to be aware of what is going on, what the impact might be on them and the key concepts of Lean and how they might be able to get involved. Over time this group should disappear as more and more people become involved in Lean events and activities.

PRISM Step 2: Roadmap

Having prepared your organisation for Lean, you will need to Roadmap how your critical pathways and processes will operate 'in the Future' fundamentally this phase is concerned with 'designing a realistic Future State' using Value Stream Analysis Events (VSE).

You should also not forget that during this step you will also need to continue the development and communication activities within your organisation.

In this section we will specifically look at how you might run a 'Value Stream Analysis Event' (VSE):

Value Stream Analysis Event (VSE)

An example programme of activity for a Value Stream Analysis Event (VSE) is given in the Appendix. The programme is split into three phases as defined below:

- **Pre-VSE Phase** – This is where the data is gathered to support the programme, and the team are trained and prepared for the improvement process.

- **The VSE** – This is where the event occurs (and the 'Future State' is designed) with the bulk of activity undertaken in three key steps as defined earlier and repeated below:

  - Understand the Current State

  - Create a 'Blue Sky' State

  - Design a realistic 'Future State'

- **Post-VSE Phase** – This is where the implementation plan to move from the 'Current State' to the 'Future State' is finalised and communicated to the wider team as well as when the first implementation events are planned.

PRISM Step 3: Implementation

The next step in the PRISM process is to convert the concepts
in your 'Future State' into tangible improvements. It is at this
stage that you might consider using 'Rapid Improvement Events'
(also known as Kaizen Breakthrough Events, Transformation
Events etc) as well as other structures/activities such as:

- **Rapid Planning Events (RPE)** – also known as a 2P event,
  this is an intense event designed to 'de-risk' a key
  area/process prior to implementation of improvements
  and normally consists of putting together detailed plans
  for the implementation and testing/simulation of the
  concepts to ensure they work.

- **Focused Improvement Teams (FIT)** – also called a 'Task
  & Finish' team, this structure is used to implement
  improvements over a longer period by tasking a team
  to get together regularly to work on a problem. My
  recommendation is to use this type of team after
  you have made a few improvements using Rapid
  Improvement Events (RIE) or similar as you will improve
  the chance that the team will be successful.

- **Project Teams** – Used to tackle bigger projects (such as
  the introduction of a new IT system or a new building)
  that cannot be solved via a Rapid Improvement Event.

In this section I will discuss Rapid Improvement and Planning
Events as well as Focused Improvement Teams.

Rapid Improvement Events (RIE)

A Rapid Improvement Event (RIE) is used to physically improve a process in a structured manner and will normally focus on a specific area within a Pathway (or Value Stream). When people struggle to understand what types of activities could be grouped into an RIE, I normally tell them that if the problem can be solved by a 'group of brains' working together for a few days then it is suitable for an RIE. If it will take longer it is probably a Project and if people take a deep breath before answering then it will normally require a Rapid Planning Event (RPE) first.

An RIE could last between 1 and 5 days and normally consists of three phases as described below:

- **Pre-RIE Phase** – gathering data, preparing the area and team for the improvement event

- **The RIE** – the physical implementation of improvements and normally following the sequence of activities defined below:

    - **Opening Brief** – given by a senior manager/director to help motivate the team

    - **Understand Current State** – working to understand how the process works in detail

    - **Design New Solution/s** – designing solutions that introduce 'Flow' and 'Pull'

    - **Implement & Test New Solution** – moving items into position and then testing it works as expected

- **Planning for Sustainability** – including putting in place 'Standard Work' and also a process to audit and continuously improve the new process and a Control Board of some form (often grouped together and termed 'Leader Standard Work')

- **Closing Brief** – this is a short presentation given by the team to the managers and others with an interest in the process and which focuses on their activities and achievements.

○ **Post-RIE Phase** – testing, improving and embedding the improvements and continuing to audit the process to make sure it does not slip back

Rapid Planning Events (RPE)

Some processes are too high risk to move straight to a Rapid Improvement Event (RIE). The RPE (Rapid Planning Event) is an intermediate activity between a VSE and an RIE and is designed to 'de-risk' a process.

The RPE (which may also be termed 2P – Process Planning) can last between 1 and 5 days (depending on the issues being tackled) and normally consists of three phases as described below.

○ **Pre-RPE Phase** – gathering data, preparing the area and team for the planning event

○ **The RPE** – the RPE process normally consists of the following steps:

- **Opening Brief** – given by a senior manager/director to help motivate the team

- **Understand Current State** – working to understand how the process works in detail

- **Design & Test New Solution/s** – designing solutions that introduce 'Flow' and 'Pull' and testing that these solutions are feasible and will work as expected

- **Planning for Implementation** – putting together the detailed implementation plan

- **Closing Brief** – this is a short presentation given by the team to the managers and others with an interest in the process and which focuses on their activities and achievements.

- **Planning & Implementation Phase** – preparing for the resulting improvement event (RIE)

Focused Improvement Teams (FIT)

A Focused Improvement Team (also known as a Task & Finish Group) is a team focused on a specific problem or issue where it is not appropriate to use a Rapid Improvement Event.

Closing Comments

Whilst the three steps of PRISM identified in this section will go a long way to ensuring that you avoid many of the CRITICAL mistakes, we need to recognise that this is a further two steps involved in embedding Lean into a process and these

are described in outline below and in more detail in our book
'Sustaining Lean Healthcare Programmes:

- **PRISM Step 4: Sustaining Improvement** – an essential
  step designed to convert changes in 'processes' into
  changes in behaviour

- **PRISM Step 5: Maintaining Momentum** – having overcome
  inertia and implemented the 'Future State', this step
  is concerned with setting the direction for the next
  improvement phase in the pathway, recognising that
  Lean is a journey and not a destination

Your Top Points From This Chapter

◐
....

◐
....

◐
....

◐
....

◐
....

Chapter 4

Lean at different organisational levels

Lean is a flexible approach to improvement and can be applied at different organisational levels. Each level creates different problems and stresses and this short chapter details the three most common levels at which Lean can be introduced and what to look out for when making improvements at that level.

Organisation Level

The highest level at which Lean can be introduced is at the Organisation (or Enterprise) level. This is where an organisation looks to go lean across all functions and in all areas, becoming a 'Lean Healthcare Organisation'. Successful achievement of this will create massive improvements in organisational performance as well as a complete culture shift but it is time and resource intensive and can take some years to implement fully (although you will make lots of gains along the way). The Pro & Con arguments for introducing Lean at the Organisation Level are shown below.

Pro	Con
O Can create a culture of improvement O Makes improvement across all pathways O Biggest impact on the organisation O Fundamentally challenges all assumptions O Motivating for staff to be involved in	O Easily derailed in the early stages O Resource intensive O Requires long-term management commitment

Pathway Level

Introducing Lean at the Pathway Level is where the focus is on an 'End to End' (E2E) pathway. This is a much easier level to introduce Lean as it is less resource intensive and can achieve quick results. It still requires management commitment and the allocation of resources, as well as a focus on how each pathway impacts on other pathways. The Pro & Con arguments for introducing Lean at the Pathway Level are shown below.

Pro	Con
O Quicker to introduce than organisational level O End to end improvement in key pathways O Less resource intensive O Creates real life case studies of improvement	O May not result in fundamental culture change O Still requires significant management input O Can result in fragmented improvements

Process Level

Introducing Lean at the Process Level looks to make improvements within specific departments or areas. This is the easiest and quickest level to introduce improvements but brings with it the greatest risk of simply transferring problems upstream or downstream in a pathway. To illustrate this I have provided a short example based on a Pathway (Value Stream) in Emergency Admissions which has been simplified to consist of four key areas as shown below:

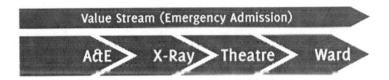

At the Process Level, you would look to introduce Lean in one of the departments (say X-Ray) in isolation of the other areas. This would minimise the number of people who would need to be involved (and the number of departments who would need to be represented) but could simply result in problems or risk being transferred elsewhere in the Pathway.

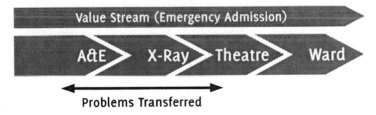

For example, a radiology focused improvement to (say) eliminate ring fenced trauma slots might increase capacity for the local team but increase the risk to trauma patients requiring an urgent slot

The Pro & Con arguments for introducing Lean at the Process Level are shown below.

Pro	Con
○ Quick to implement	○ Can lead to fragmented improvements
○ Minimal resource required	
	○ Little or no impact on overall culture
○ Useful for testing out Lean as a concept	
	○ Can create additional organisational risks elsewhere in the process
○ Useful for small scale issues and problems	

Your Top Points From This Chapter

○

....

○

....

○

....

○

....

○

....

Chapter 5

Thinking Lean

This chapter looks at some of the additional thinking that underpins successful Lean improvement programmes and also helps to start you thinking about Lean terminology in your organisation.

Planned & Emergent Work

In Lean terminology, activity that can be predicted is called 'Planned Work' and activity that cannot be planned is called 'Emergent Work'. Some assumptions can be made about the percentages of time spent on Planned and Emergent work respectively and it may even be possible to determine how long each piece of Emergent Work might take to deal with depending on previous trends and analysis.

Runner, Repeater & Stranger

Another important Lean idea that we have already encountered is the frequency with which events within the organisation occur (I am using the term events here meaning occurrences/ activities rather than 'Lean Events'). Activities are categorised as 'Runners, Repeaters and Strangers':

- ▷ A Runner is an activity or event that occurs 'frequently' (often daily)

- ▷ A Repeater is something that occurs less regularly, but is still something the team are familiar with seeing (often it occurs weekly or at most monthly)

- ▷ A Stranger is something that occurs only rarely (say, less frequently than once per month)

Takt Time

Takt Time is a very important concept in Lean as it defines the 'beat rate' of a process, meaning the frequency that a 'customer' demands something from the process.

It is calculated as follows: **Available Time/Demand Rate**

An example Takt Time calculation is shown below:

The A&E Department is open 24 Hours Per Day and in that time will deal with (on average) 480 people, therefore the Takt Time would be: (24Hrsx60)/480 = 3 Minutes. This means that 'On Average' the process is triggered every three minutes by the arrival of a patient.

Obviously, in a real project we would look at demand over time (to look for patterns of demand such as peaks on Friday nights etc).

Manual Cycle Time and Lead Time

From the moment an activity is triggered (or the previous activity ends) the clock starts ticking on the next activity and it stops ticking when the activity is completed. This total elapsed time is called the 'Lead Time' (or alternatively Cycle Time).

For example, if a patient arrives at outpatients at 9am and leaves at 11.30am the total elapsed time (the Lead Time) will be 2 hours 30 minutes. If during this period, they are weighed (5 minutes), have a blood pressure check (10 minutes) and a consultation (15 Minutes) the total 'activity' (the Processing or Touch Time) will be 30 minutes.

Pull Signals

In Lean terms a Pull Signal is when a customer (or someone involved in delivering the process) requests activity to be undertaken – in that they 'Pull' resources towards them.

A Pull Signal could be directly visual (as in a light on switchboard when someone calls in), indirectly visual (as in when a storage bin becomes empty and therefore 'demands' a replenishment) or physical (the customer arrives at A&E).

In an ideal Lean system, no activity would occur unless a customer demands it. In manufacturing environments they will often 'build to stock' but luckily in Healthcare, it is not often possible to 'stack' items or undertake work in advance of requirement, although batching (calls, patients, paperwork) is very common and therefore I have included the concept of 'Pull' as a possible way of avoiding batching.

'5 Second Rule'

The 5 Second Rule is something that is generally created using the 5S+1 Tool (see later) and which, put simply, means:

> "An informed person walking into an area should
> be able to know enough about the process
> to remain safe, know where things are and
> to understand what is happening in under 5
> Seconds"

How often do people come into the office, ward or department and spend ages trying to determine what the current status is? Whether that is the backlog of calls, the availability of swabs or the location of staff, it is often a very large percentage of the total working day. This is very wasteful of resources and leads to numerous errors and mistakes and the aim of the '5 Second Rule' is to eliminate these problems and through this improve effectiveness.

Going to Gemba

An important concept when undertaking Lean Activities is to 'Walk the Process' and 'Go to Gemba' (which means going to the place where things happen). This allows you to see exactly what happens, to take real timings and to avoid the pitfall of 'guessing' what actually happens.

Trying to map and improve processes whilst in an office remote to the actual area where the work is done often results in maps which are inaccurate by up to 50% as people forget steps and underestimate the amount of time and effort required for activities.

Corporate Projects, Improvement Events & Go Do Its!

Not everything that arises during a Lean programme can be fixed by, or needs, an Improvement Event (RIE/RPE etc) to fix it and the outcomes of a VSE will include a mix of Projects, Events and Do Its.

For larger issues (such as the introduction of a new IT System or similar) it may require some months of planning, numerous decisions and various committees to be convened. As such, these 'Corporate Projects' will normally need to be addressed via a different approach than the RIE/RPE approach proposed earlier.

For small issues, things that are completely obvious and do not need any form of decision to be taken (what might be termed a 'No Brainer') these just require people to get on and 'Go Do It!' (this normally includes simples things like putting in new paperwork or changing a protocol, essentially activities that can be undertaken by one person without referring to anyone else in the organisation).

Your Top Points From This Chapter

Chapter 6

Key Lean Tools & Concepts

In this section, I have pulled out the top six tools that I believe will make the biggest impact on Healthcare Organisations. I have avoided providing pages and pages of details tools that you might never use and have focused on providing a very quick introduction to the tools that will be of most use during your first year of Lean.

In addition, at the end of this chapter, I have provided a short summary of some of the other tools and concepts that will help your Lean programme go further and faster.

The Top Six Lean Tools & Concepts

Key Tool/Concept 1: 5S+1

5S+1 is a process designed to create a 'Visual Workplace', which is somewhere that is safe, organised and which conforms to the '5 Second Rule'. 5S+1 is often confused by some people as being a 'tidy up' but in fact 5S+1 is a systematic way of managing a process to reduce the effort required to manage the process and the risk to staff and customers.

The steps involved in undertaking a 5S+1 exercise are shown in the figure below:

▷ **Sort** – remove unwanted items from the area to reduce clutter

▷ **Set** – set what remains in order and give each item a marked 'home location'

▷ **Shine** – keep the area clean and return items to their 'home location' at the ends of shifts etc

▷ **Standardise** – define the responsibilities of Teams & Managers in maintaining standards

▷ **Sustain** – audit and improve the area

▷ **Safety (+1)** – at each step, ensure you are not making decisions detrimental to safety

An example 5S+1 Audit Form can be found in the Appendix.

Key Tool/Concept 2: Standard Work

Standard Work defines the most efficient methods required to undertake work with the available equipment, people and material. At its simplest, Standard Work involves a group agreeing the most efficient way to undertake a process and then having them follow that process until it is agreed to change/improve it further. To get to a 'Standard' process requires the current process to be analysed and then structured to minimise 'Non Value Adding' activity and maximise safety. Standard work therefore uses a range of tools and documentation including:

▷ **Method Sheets** – how the process/activity is undertaken

▷ **Layout Sheets** – how the area is to be laid out

▷ **Loading Charts** – how the work is broken down between individuals

▷ **Leader Standard Work** – how to audit/monitor/support the area for continuous improvement

Key Tool/Concept 3: Flow

We have already encountered flow earlier in this book when we covered the '5 Principles of Lean'. Flow is concerned with eliminating delays between stages and enabling processes to achieve 'One Piece Flow' that is emphasised below. In the example shown we have a 'batch' process where ten items need to be processed through 4 Steps (A, B, C & D). All 10 items are done at Step A and then passed to Step B where all ten are done before being passed on, and so on.

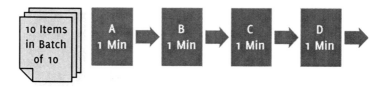

The impact of this 'batching' is that the first item is not completed at Step D until 31 Minutes after the start of the process and the last arrives at 40 Minutes after the start.

If we contrast this with a process that 'Flows' (technically called One Piece Flow), where items are passed 'one at a time' from Step A to Step B and so on, then the following is the result:

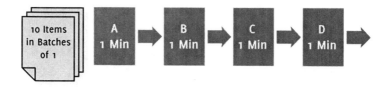

The first item is received out from Step D in 4 Minutes and the last in 13 Minutes, a reduction of 66% in the Lead Time against the 'batch' example.

Making a process 'Flow' is about removing barriers between steps (physical, cultural etc), moving steps closer together and setting up each step so that it can perform its task without stopping.

Key Tool/Concept 4: Pull Systems

A 'Pull' System (also known as a Kanban System) is a system that triggers activity 'on demand' – with the aim of ensuring that work is not done before it is required and that is occurs at the right time to ensure the process keeps 'flowing'.

Pull systems can be used to improve 'flow' through Theatre, control consumables or even trigger paperwork to be produced. Two simple pull systems are described below.

'In one Pull System, the arrival of a set of patient notes in a 'Discharge Required' container could be used to 'trigger' the production of a discharge summary.

Another example Pull System uses a 'Two Container' system as shown below. As the first blue container is emptied the yellow container slides forward and its appearance acts as a trigger for further parts to be ordered prior to the process 'running out' of parts.

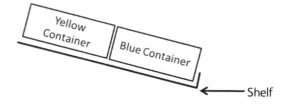

Shelf

Key Tool/Concept 5: SMED (Single Minute Exchange of Die) – (aka 'Set Up Reduction')

The concept of SMED is that it should never take longer than 9 minutes (hence Single Minute) to change over from one activity to the next, whether that is the time from the end of one operation to the start of the next, or the end of one clinic appointment to the start of the next.

The standard analogy of how you achieve this reduction in changeover times is to compare the changing of tyres in Formula 1 racing with doing it at home, and I have shown this below.

Example of home changeover:	Example of Formula 1 changeover:
○ Search for car keys	○ Inform 'pit team' you are 'coming in'
○ Try to dig out jack, tools etc	○ Park in yellow box
○ Read manual to determine where to put jack	○ Slide under jack and raise car
○ Read manual to check how to remove wheel	○ Release wheel nuts (1 per wheel)
○ Find wheel locking nut in glove box	○ Put on new wheels
○ Have a cup of tea	○ Drop car back onto ground
○ Locate jack and pump up car	○ Drive away
○ Struggle to remove wheel nuts	
○ Pull off wheel and put on new wheel	
○ Struggle to lock wheel nuts again	
○ Lower car	
Total Elapsed Time: 1 Hour?	Total Elapsed Time: 8 Seconds

The difference in Formula 1 is that they have got all the equipment in place prior to the car coming into the pits, they have designed the process to make it easy to remove the wheels, the team have trained to work together and the process has been standardised to make it easy to follow for everyone and reduce both risk and time.

SMED (Set Up Reduction), has significant applications in Theatre Changeovers and Clinic Changeovers.

Key Tool/Concept 6: Poka Yoke (Mistake Proofing)

The last of the six key tools I believe will make the biggest difference is Poka Yoke, namely the process of designing out problems and issues and making it difficult for people to make mistakes. The classic example that people in the UK will be familiar with is of a three pin electric plug. There is no way that a normal user can insert the plug into a socket in any other way than the correct way (without a mallet).

The three pin plug has been designed to be 'Mistake Proof'. It is not always possible to completely redesign a process so we may have to use different approaches to 'mistake proofing' a process and Poka Yoke uses the following 'hierarchy' of how to mistake proof a process.

- Eliminate the problem by designing out the problem/ step/process

- If you can't eliminate it, can you Replace it by installing a safer process/step?

- If you can't replace it, can you Redesign it to reduce the risk of problems arising?

- If you can't redesign it, can you Reduce the risk of it going wrong?

- If you can't reduce the risk, can you Detect the problem more quickly?

○ If you can't detect the problem, can you Mitigate the problem/risk to reduce costs of problems?

Obviously, as you move 'down' the list, the impact becomes less and I would urge you to focus on the first three steps listed above as these will generate the best (and safest) impact.

Other Tools of Lean

Although I have introduced my top six tools list and believe that these will cover the majority of the tools required during the first year of your Lean programme, I have included a very brief overview of some of the other tools of Lean that you might encounter as you progress on your journey.

TPM (Total Productive Maintenance)

TPM (Total Productive Maintenance) is a concept whereby front-line teams are given responsibility for day to day servicing of the processes/equipment they use (called Autonomous Maintenance). The principle is that empowering front line teams to manage the routine 'servicing' of their process frees management time and reduces the number of occasions when the process/equipment fails completely.

Heijunka

Heijunka is all about putting in place systems to level the activity in a process to avoid peaks and troughs and has lots of useful applications within Healthcare environments including reducing demand and mix variation in administration, pharmacy, pathology etc.

String Diagram (aka Spaghetti Diagrams)

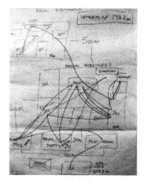

This is an extremely useful tool for mapping how people and information move around an area. The idea is to imagine the person (or information) is being dragged around with paint on its feet – and you will be a picture like the one below:

An example string diagram

FMEA (Failure Modes & Effects Analysis)

FMEA (Failure Modes & Effects Analysis) creates a priority list for addressing risks/issues in a process by multiplying level of risk. An example FMEA Form is shown in the Appendix.

Backbone & Ribs

The Backbone and Ribs is created during a Rapid Planning Event (RPE) and shows, for each process step, the six key 'ribs' that need to be in place to enable the process to function, these being: Information/IT, Documents, People, Equipment, Materials and Tools.

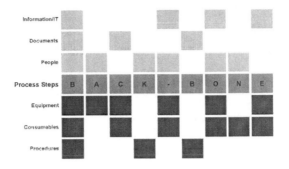

An example 'Backbone & Ribs' Chart

Try Its

Sometimes called 'Cardboard Engineering', a 'Try It' exercise is used to physically measure an area to ensure the new layout will work and to identify any risks that may occur during the implementation stage.

Paper Layout

A Paper Layout is used to plan how an area will be laid out prior to actually moving anything. It can be used in any form of Lean Event and is also best used with a 'Try It'.

5 Whys (Root Cause Analysis)

5 Whys is a simple tool used to help identify the root cause of a problem. It relies on asking the question 'Why' five times, with the idea being that the root cause will be exposed by the time of the fifth question as shown below:

Problem: Patient Not Called As Promised

○ Why 1 - Why did the Patient not get called back?

○ Why 2 - Why did their name not appear on the 'to call' list?

○ Why 3 - Why were their details not in the folder?

○ Why 4 - Why was the standard form not used?

○ Why 5 - Why did we not induct 'X' correctly? (Root Cause)

Pareto Analysis

Pareto Analysis is a technique that works on the 80/20 rule which is an assumption that 80% of the problems/issues are caused by only 20% of the causes or activities.

SPC (Statistical Process Control)

SPC (Statistical Process Control) is a tool frequently used in Lean and Six Sigma projects to monitor the performance of a process to measure variance and to spot trends that could indicate a problem or dangerous activity prior to it occurring.

Fishbone Diagrams (Ishikawa Diagrams)

Fishbone Diagrams, also known as 'Cause & Effect Diagrams) is a creative tool used to identify the primary causes of a problem (effect). The causes are often categorised by the '4Ms' of Materials, Men, Machines and Methods.

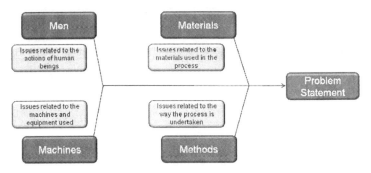

A stylised view of a 'Fishbone Diagram'

Hand-Off Chart

A Hand-Off Chart lists the departments involved in a process and shows how information and customers move around the process. A line is drawn each time a piece of information or a patient is 'handed off' to someone else in the process and the resulting chart is excellent for visually highlighting faulty processes.

An example Hand-Off Chart

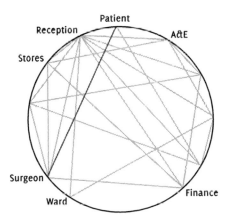

Process Analysis

A standard tool for understanding how processes work, and
something that many people confuse with a 'Lean Project'. For
each step you might want to gather additional data using 'data
tickets' as shown below.

STEP NUMBER	12
Start of Process	Arrival of paperwork
End of Process	Paperwork completed
Elapsed (Lead) Time	10 Hrs 15 Mins
Work (Process) Time	15 Mins
No of People	3
Key Risks	Nil
% Right 1st Time	74%
Problems with Step	Paperwork arrives badly formatted and difficult to read leading to lost time

A rule of thumb about Process Mapping is to ensure that there
are between 50 and 100 'Steps' for any process – of whatever
length! Below 50 and there is insufficient data to make informed
decision and above 100 there is too much time required to
complete the form (and too much detail to make informed
decisions). If possible, map at least one Runner, Repeater and
Stranger activity for each pathway being looked at – and choose
the 'most likely' activity that will occur at each step.

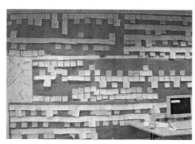

An example Process Map

20+ Improvements

A very simple tool that helps teams to 'see' the problems in the process they are looking at. When they are looking at a process ask the team to find a minimum of 20 things that could be improved. It will be surprising what they suggest!

Future State Map

Creating the 'Future State' Map is one of the last things done during a VSE and contains a picture of how the new process will work in the 'Future'. It uses standardised pictures (as can be seen in the Appendix).

An example 'Future State' Map

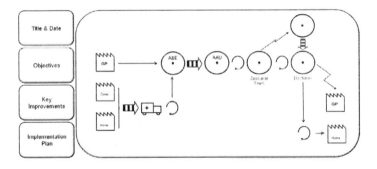

Jidoka (aka Autonomation)

Jidoka is often referred to as 'automation with a human face' and is the concept of empowering teams to stop the line when they spot problems so that they can be fixed and over time selectively automating the identification and elimination of problems.

Lean Tools Matrix

In the following table I have tried to show when you might use the tools covered in this chapter:

Lean Tool Matrix	Redesign Phase (VSE)	Improvement Events (RIE)	Planning Events (RPE)
5S+1		✓	
String Diagram	✓	✓	✓
Processing Mapping	✓	✓	✓
Future State Map	✓		
Standard Work		✓	
Pull Systems		✓	
FMEA	✓	✓	✓
Backbone & Ribs			✓
Paper Layout		✓	✓
Try It		✓	✓
5 Whys (Root Cause Analysis)	✓	✓	✓
Pareto Analysis	✓	✓	✓
Fishbone Diagram	✓	✓	✓
SMED		✓	
TPM		✓	
Heijunka		✓	
Jidoka		✓	

Your Top Points From This Chapter

○

○

○

○

○

Chapter 7

The top 10 problems with Lean

In this chapter, I have listed the 10 most common problems that Practitioners will find with the implementation of Lean programmes. In my book 'Sustaining Lean Healthcare Programmes' I explore further issues that arise with Lean projects and suggest how you can put in place management systems to avoid them occurring.

1. Confusing Lean with Process Mapping

A lot of your team will have tried Process Mapping (and the resulting tinkering with the process that this leads too without a formal 'Future State') and will think of this as Lean. Once they have experienced a Value Stream Analysis Event (VSE), this perception will go away very quickly but until then you will have to smile when the team moan that they do not want to do 'process mapping' again.

2. Failing to move from discussion to action

A lot of organisational inertia surrounds previous programmes which failed to move from 'doing improvement on paper' to actually implementing the improvements. Creating some 'quick wins' will overcome this issue very quickly.

3. Not dealing with roadblocks effectively

As you progress through your improvement activities you will encounter 'roadblocks', these being things that people put in front of you to prevent the team moving forward and you will need to spend some time trying to decipher what are real problems that you need to deal with and which are just diversions. There are a couple of useful sayings which might help you in this matter:

- **"It is better to achieve 80% now rather than 100% never."** – meaning it is better to implement a solution that makes 80% of occurrences better rather than trying to design a solution that is completely 'ideal' as you will never move from discussion into action.

- **"Design for the most likely solution and you will have more time to deal with the exceptions."** – This statement suggests you design your process/pathway to operate within the most likely limits or to cope with the most likely maximum and minimum volumes and you will eliminate most of the problems and have much more time to deal with exceptional circumstances.

4. Leading from the Middle

Without the support of an Improvement Sponsor, you are literally wasting your time doing Lean – it is impossible to implement and sustain improvements without top level support so treat that as your number 1 priority. You should also consider how you will 'Manage for Daily Improvements' and this is achieved by what is termed 'Leader Standard Work'. Different levels of Leaders need to undertake specific activities. Supervisors need to maintain Control Boards and do regular audits, as well as leading regular Continuous Improvement Sessions. Senior managers need to 'walk the boards and the wards', speak to front-line teams and gather an understanding of what is going on and chair improvement groups on occasions.

5. Failing to 'Follow Up'

Having implemented changes it is essential to keep some focus on ensuring that the process does not 'slip back'. This requires management input (again Leader Standard Work comes into this) and team audits for a number of weeks after the changes have been implemented.

6. Failing to deal with the genuine concerns of the team

When a Lean programme is announced everyone will immediately think about 'WIIFM' (What's in it for me?) This does not mean that they start thinking about money, but they might worry about their jobs, whether they will be humiliated by being picked out of the crowd and so on. It is important that people understand exactly why the changes are needed (which is covered by undertaking a Scoping Session) and what (if anything) it means to them.

7. Failing to Scope the improvement properly

Aircraft need a 'flight plan' to tell them about their flight and organisations need a map to plan the implementation of Lean. Failing to set out a planned journey for your Lean project from the start is a key way to make it go wrong, waste time/effort and tackle the wrong issues.

8. Not allocating sufficient resources

There is no magic bullet for Lean and many organisations think that it can be achieved by being an additional task slotted into the diary of busy people. Lean requires long-term investment, management involvement and the release of people to participate to be successful.

9. Putting out conflicting messages

It is important to be clear from the start about why the organisation is implementing Lean and what you are expecting to get out of the process (and why). Changing messages reduces the importance people attach to Lean and end up killing it!

10. Undertaking inappropriate training

Lean is learnt best by doing – so don't spend too long doing training on topics that may never be used prior to actually implementing something! It will wear people out and defeat the purpose of your Lean activity.

Your Top Points From This Chapter

○
....

○
....

○
....

○
....

○
....

About the Author

Mark Eaton *MSc MBA CEng FRSA*

Starting his career as a Design Engineer working on the design of missiles, Mark subsequently branched out into manufacturing where he held a number of senior roles in blue chip manufacturing organisations in the defence, aerospace and media industries, working to introduce Lean Concepts in the years before Lean was called 'Lean'.

Latterly, Mark moved into consultancy and was involved in a number of high profile regional and national Lean Programmes for various public organisations, including the DTi's flagship Lean Transformation Programme in a number of UK Regions. For his work, Mark was awarded the Viscount Nuffield Medal in 2004 for his contribution to UK Industry.

In addition to extensive experience of Lean in manufacturing, Mark has also led significant transformations within the Armed Forces and wider public sector before finding a passion for working within the Healthcare Sector where he has worked across entire health economies and provided strategic level advice to SHAs and organisations such as the NPSA.

Mark is a Chartered Engineer and is the Chair of the Institute for Engineering & Technology's Manufacturing Professional Network and a member of their Healthcare Executive Team. In addition to having over 50 published articles on topics related to innovation, Lean and sustainable improvement, Mark has also helped write a number of public policy documents, including both regional Innovation and Manufacturing Strategies and he continues to provide advice and support to a variety of institutes and public bodies.

Mark is also co-author of Sustaining Lean Healthcare Programmes.

Appendix 1

Lean Dictionary

2P:
(aka Rapid Planning Events) Standing for Process Planning, 2P is the process of preparing an area or organisation for improvement and often used to 'de-risk' a process prior to implementation. Related to 3P (various definitions but most commonly Production Process Planning that is used to develop new products, processes and services).

4 M's:
(see also Ishikawa diagram (cause & effect diagram)). 4Ms are the main categories used to assess the causes of 'issues' (effects), namely Material, Method, Machine, Man.

5 Principles:
The 5 Principles of Lean as first defined by 'Womack & Jones' in their book 'Lean Thinking' and standing for 'Value, Value Stream, Flow, Pull, Perfection'.

5 Second Rule:
A key concept of the 'Visual Workplace' in that problems/issues/status are visible to an informed person in under 5 Seconds.

5 Why's:
(aka Root Cause Analysis) The process of asking "Why?" 5 times to uncover the potential root cause of problems that have been encountered.

5S+1: The process used to create a 'Visual Workplace' that is safe and effective. The steps are Sort, Set, Shine, Standardise, Sustain (5S) and Safety (+1).

7 Wastes (+1): (aka WORMPIT) The seven main 'Wastes' (or Non-Value Adding activity), plus the waste of 'Talent', namely; Waiting, Over Processing (Production), Rework, Motion, Transport, Processing Waste, Inventory and Talent.

ABC Analysis: Volume based groupings used to segment part numbers in order to define the inventory policy that they fall within.

Andon: A visual system (often a light) that provides a signal to managers/supervisors when abnormalities occur within processes.

Autonomation: (see also Jidoka) Sometimes referred too as "automation with a human touch" , this is the process of automatically stopping processes rather than allowing large amounts of scrap (or lots of problems) to build up.

Autonomous Maintenance: A concept from TPM (Total Productive Maintenance) where the 'operator' takes responsibility for basic maintenance and servicing of the equipment they use to reduce 'down time'.

Batch Processing: The process of undertaking work (such as processing patients or producing products) in 'batches' and is the antithesis of 'One Piece Flow'.

Cells: An arranged collection of people, equipment, machines, materials and methods such that activities occur in sequence with minimum waste and so that the area can achieve 'Continuous Flow'.

Chaku-Chaku: (aka Load-Load) Used in one piece flow systems (ideally where machines automatically unload parts) so that a worker can rapidly move a part through a process from one machine to the next without having to unload parts.

Continuous Flow: (aka One Piece Flow) A process where items are processed and moved one 'piece' at a time, ideally in a process where one item is completed just before the next part of the process requires it.

Cycle Time: (aka Lead Time) The total time from the start to the end of a process or alternatively (in some text) the average time between completed items or patients coming out of the end of the process.

Demand: The frequency with which services/products need to be produced based on 'Customer Demand'.

FIFO: Standing for 'First In, First Out', this is the process of dealing with activities strictly in the sequence that they are presented at the 'front door'.

Flow: The process of arranging activities such that bottlenecks, delays between stages and other losses are minimised and the process is capable of 'Continuous Flow'.

Gemba: A Japanese term meaning "the actual place" where value is added (such as a Clinic/Theatre or Shop-Floor).

Hand-Off Chart: A diagrammatic representation of a process showing how information/products/ patients etc are 'handed off' from one person to another.

Heijunka: The process of levelling demand in variation and mix of product/activity over a fixed time period.

Jishuken: A Japanese word used to describe a "hands-on knowledge workshop."

Jidoka: (see Autonomation).

Kaikaku: (another name for Rapid Improvement Events) A process of 'radical improvements', also called such things as 'Step Change' and 'Breakthrough', and forming the basis of Rapid Improvement

Events.

Kalzen: (also commonly thought of a Continuous Improvement) Kaizen comes from the Japanese for "to improve for the better" in incremental steps.

Kaizen Event: (aka Rapid Improvement Event) See Kaikaku.

Kanban: (aka Pull) Kanban means 'signal' and Kanban is used to trigger demand for an activity, product or service.

Kanban Post: A storage container for Kanban cards that are 'signalling' the need for a product/ service to be delivered.

Lead-Time: The total elapsed time from the start to the end of a 'process' (ie Clock Start to Clock Stop). Including the sum of all Value Adding and Non-Value Adding time.

Leader Standard Work: The activities undertaken by supervisors and/or managers to sustain and maintain the benefits achieved through Rapid Improvement Events, including Control Boards, MBWA and Audits (including a 5S+1 Audit)

Lean: A business improvement strategy based on the Toyota Production System and designed to eliminate 'waste' and improve effectiveness in processes.

Machine Cycle Time: The total time taken to process an item or patient on a piece of equipment.

MBWA: Standing for 'Management By Walking About' and being the process of managers showing interest in processes and finding solutions by 'going to Gemba' and interacting with staff and customers.

Mistake Proofing: See Poka-Yoke.

Muda: (aka Waste) The Japanese word for 'Non-Value Adding Activity'.

Mura: A Japanese word meaning variation or fluctuation.

Muri: A Japanese work used to mean 'overburdening' or 'unreasonableness'.

Nemawashi: From a Japanese expression meaning to 'prepare the ground for planting', this is used to describe the practice of engaging people and gaining 'buy in' for the change process.

Non-Value-Added Activity (NVA): (aka Waste and Muda) An activity that uses up time, cost, resources or space but does not add value to the product / activity itself. Normally identified as things that the customer does not 'value' and would not pay for (if they had to).

One Piece Flow: See Continuous Flow.

Overall Equipment Effectiveness (OEE): A measure used within TPM (Total Productive Maintenance) to describe how effectively equipment (or a Process) is being used and is calculated by multiplying the % availability rate by the % performance rate by the % quality rate.

Overproduction (Over-Processing): The worst form of 'waste' or Non-Value Adding activity is to produce more things than are needed or do more work than is required.

Pacemaker: A part of a process that is a bottleneck and needs to be scheduled to ensure the smooth flow of the rest of the process.

Plan, Do, Study, Act (PDSA): A modified form of PDCA (Plan, Do, Check, Act) first defined by Deming in the 1950's. PDSA is the form used in Healthcare.

Pitch: The amount of time required by an area to go through one cycle of work (and produce one 'container' of products or outputs) and calculated by multiplying Takt time by the quantity of activity done in each 'pack'.

Poka-Yoke: (aka Mistake Proofing) The process of designing out (or mitigating) the risk of problems arising in a process.

Processing Time: The total manual time for an activity to be undertaken.

Pull:	See Kanban, but also used as a term to mean 'to draw materials/equipment/people to me' in opposition to a 'Push System' (see below).
Push:	The production of goods, or 'push' of activity, irrespective of the ability of the downstream process to 'consume' the product or activity.
Rapid Improvement Event (RIE):	See Kaikaku.
Rapid Planning Event (RPE):	See 2P
Runner, Repeater, Stranger:	Runners are activities undertaken 'regularly' (normally everyday), Repeaters are common activities that occur less frequently than Runners (say weekly to monthly) and Strangers are activities that come up rarely. In addition, sometimes the term 'Alien' is added to Runner, Repeater, Stranger, to indicate completely unexpected activities.
Safety Stock:	Material held to compensate for variations in the process and in supply.
Sensei:	Meaning 'Teacher' in Japanese and normally applied to people with a deep understanding of Lean.

Set-Up Time: The amount of time required to 'changeover' a process and measured from the end of the last activity of type 'A' until the first good activity undertaken of type 'B'.

Single Minute Exchange of Die (SMED):   A process designed to reduce setup or changeover times and therefore the creation of a 'Continuous Flow' system.

String Diagram: (aka Spaghetti Diagram) A chart tracing a line showing the path taken by a product of person during an activity or process.

Standard Work: The process of formerly defining the work method, the tools, staff, quality, inventory and sequence of activities undertaken in a process.

Supermarket: A stack of parts (or patients) used to supply an area or process.

Takt Time: Meaning 'beat rate', Takt Time is the rate of demand by customers for activity or products and is calculated by dividing Available Time (ie the hours worked per day or shift) by the rate of Customer Orders or Demand.

Total Productive Maintenance (TPM):   A process for improving efficiency by eliminating the down-time in a process through activities such as 'Autonomous Maintenance'.

Toyota Production System (TPS):	The production system developed by the Toyota Motor Company that focuses on the elimination of waste throughout the value stream.
Value Added Activity:	Any activity that 'transforms' the product (or patient) in some way and that is something that the 'customer' is willing to pay for (if they had too).
Value Stream Map (VSM):	A detailed process map showing all the steps involved in a process from 'End to End' (E2E).
Visual Workplace:	(aka Visualisation) The design of a work area such that the status and problems can be identified immediately and that follow the '5 Second Rule'.
Voice of the Customer (VotC):	The concept of listening to what a customer group really wants from your products and services and then designing your processes to deliver what customers see as 'value adding'.
Waste:	See Non-Value Adding Activity.
Work-in-Process (WIP):	Work that has started 'production' but have not yet completed.
WORMPIT:	See 7 Wastes+1.

Appendix 2: 5S^{+1} Audit Form

Area	Check Question	0	1	2	3	4	5
Sort	Are there unneeded items in the area?						
	Is there any equipment or other materials that are being held but not used?						
Score_____	Are there any unused documents or instruments in the area?						
	Is it obvious which items are current and in use?						
Set	Is it obvious what happens in the work areas and are control processes in place?						
	Are signs for storage places for documents and equipment in place and correct?						
Score_____	Are all shelved and stored items labelled and located correctly?						
	Are the purposes of different areas clearly marked and are they correct?						
Shine	Are the work areas and floors tidy and free of clutter?						
	Are items returned to their 'home' locations at the end of every working day or shift?						
Score_____	Are the required equipment and materials available and in good working order?						
	Do employees know their 5S+1 routine?						

Scoring
5 = Exceptional = no room for improvement
4 = Very good / could be used as best practice example
3 = Good / requirements exceeded in some areas
2 = Acceptable / requirements met
1 = More effort required to make improvements
0 = No improvement made or no evidence available

Standardise	Does everyone understand the purpose of their 5S+1 activities?						
	Is there a maintenance standard or checklist for each process and piece of equipment?						
	Is there a clear improvement plan for each area?						
Score_____	Are there clear instructions visible for how to operate the area's 5S+1 process?						
Sustain	Do employees implement the 5S+1 criteria consistently?						
	Is there a regular audit schedule to monitor 5S+1 performance?						
	Does the area leader take an active interest in 5S+1 and the actions arising?						
Score_____	Do employees & managers take action to correct low scores on the 5S+1 Audit?						
Safety	Has a risk assessment been undertaken and actioned?						
	Are required safety procedures available and in place?						
	Is there an on-going programme to look at and reduce risks in the area?						
Score_____	Are the team aware of how their role contributes to managing and reducing risk?						

Total Score (Maximum Score 120)	

Date Created & By Whom	
Area Being Audited	

Scoring
5 = Exceptional – no room for improvement
4 = Very good / could be used as best practice example
3 = Good / requirements exceeded in some areas
2 = Acceptable / requirements met
1 = More effort required to make improvements
0 = No improvement made or no evidence available

Appendix 3

Common 'Future State' Symbols

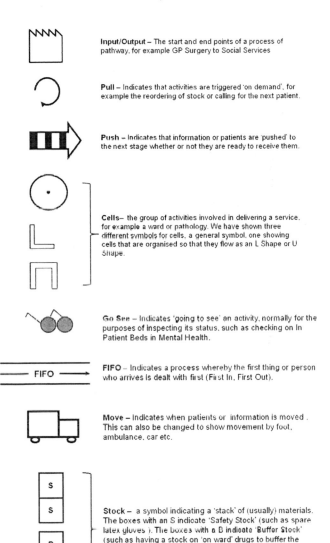

Input/Output – The start and end points of a process of pathway, for example GP Surgery to Social Services

Pull – Indicates that activities are triggered 'on demand', for example the reordering of stock or calling for the next patient.

Push – Indicates that information or patients are 'pushed' to the next stage whether or not they are ready to receive them.

Cells – the group of activities involved in delivering a service, for example a ward or pathology. We have shown three different symbols for cells, a general symbol, one showing cells that are organised so that they flow as an L Shape or U Shape.

Go See – Indicates 'going to see' an activity, normally for the purposes of inspecting its status, such as checking on In Patient Beds in Mental Health.

FIFO – Indicates a process whereby the first thing or person who arrives is dealt with first (First In, First Out).

Move – Indicates when patients or information is moved . This can also be changed to show movement by foot, ambulance, car etc.

Stock – a symbol indicating a 'stack' of (usually) materials. The boxes with an S indicate 'Safety Stock' (such as spare latex gloves). The boxes with a B indicate 'Buffer Stock' (such as having a stock on 'on ward' drugs to buffer the process and reduce delays in the administration of drugs).

Appendix 4

Example Standard Work Process Sheet

Standard Work Process Sheet

ENSURE FILES ARE STORED IN ORDER

Title:	Date Implemented:
Health Recs Storage Files	12th November

Implemented By:	Key Notes:
A Person	The files need to be stored on rack A6 located in Room 64
(Service Improvement Team)	

Appendix 5

Failure Modes & Effects Analysis (FMEA) Form

Risk Priority Number = Severity X Occurrence X Detection

Items/Process:	Notes/References:	Prepared by:
FMEA Date	Name:	
Sheet Number of	Name:	Name:

Risk Number	Potential Failure Mode	Potential Effects of Failure	Severity (1-10)	Potential Causes of Failure	Occurrence (1-10)	Current Controls	Detection (1-10)	Risk Priority Number	Notes
	sac								

Appendix 6

Example Activity Mapping Sheet

Sheet Number:									Date Created:			
		Work Value Add	Work NVA	Waiting Delayed	Waiting Stored	Moving Transport	Yield %RFT	Distance				
Step	Activity	○	□	D	△	⇨			Days	Hrs	Mins	V A?

	Days	Hrs	Mins
Total Elapsed Time (FOR THIS SHEET)			
Value Add Time (FOR THIS SHEET)			

	Days	Hrs	Mins
Cumulative Elapsed Time (ALL SHEETS)			
Cumulative Value Add Time (ALL SHEETS)			

Appendix 7

Example Scoping Meeting Agenda

A Scoping Meeting lasts 3-4 hours and the outcome is an agreed plan (or Scoping Paper) that details what you are attempting to achieve through your programme for improvement. The plan is created by a group which ideally includes representatives from all areas affected and the resulting document should be widely communicated. Experience says that an effective Scoping Paper can double the probability that your programme will achieve the outcomes you are looking for. This short document sets out how to run a Scoping Meeting.

PRIOR TO THE SCOPING MEETING	COMPLETE ✓
Agree Attendee list with a minimum of: • Project Sponsor (Director) • Process Owners (Area Managers affected) • Change Agents (any internal improvement staff who will support the project)	
Gather Background Data	
Prepare an 'Opening Statement' for the Scoping Meeting, which normally consists of: • What is the topic/issue or area that needs improvement • Why is it important to us (including any background information) • What we would like to change and by when would we like it changed	

SCOPING MEETING AGENDA	
AGENDA ITEM	DESCRIPTION
• Opening Statement	Review opening statement created prior to the event

• Open Discussion	Deal with any questions or clarification requirements
• Develop Compelling Need	Create an inspiring statement that details why this project must happen
• Fix Measures of Success	Outline 3-5 critical measures of success for the programme
• Identify 'Scenarios'	Outline scenarios which fully 'test' the pathways to be improved
• Outline who is 'In Scope'	Detail which areas (and individuals) are going to be involved FT/PT
• Outline the 'Fixed Points'	Outline the 'boundaries', risks and anything which cannot be changed
• Identify 'Key Roles'	Identify the 'Improvement Sponsor' & 'Change Agents'
• Set out your 'Activity Plan'	Set out the plan for activities associated with the project
• Fix your Communications	Identify how the 'Scoping Paper' will be communicated

AFTER THE SCOPING MEETING	COMPLETE ✓
Complete the 'Scoping Paper' and add in any missing detail	
Communicate the 'Scoping Paper'	
Plan for the 'Next Steps' in the Programme	

Appendix 8

Example Value Stream Analysis Event Agenda

A VSE (Value Stream Analysis Event) lasts 2-5 days and normally occurs after a 'Scoping Meeting' has happened. A VSE is used to first understand and then to redesign how an organisation delivers its services (and products if appropriate) in one or more critical areas. A Value Stream (also called a Pathway) is defined as all the steps involved in delivering services from one end to the other (from initial referral to patient discharge for example).

PRIOR TO THE VSE	
4 WEEKS PRIOR TO VSE	**COMPLETE ✓**
Book the room, confirm attendees and plan for any disruption that will occur	
Identify and collect data to be collected prior to the event	
Create an 'Event Pack' consisting of: • Post Its • Clear Tape • Masking Tape • Blu-Tack • Brown Paper • Rubbish Bags • Flipchart & Pens,	
Agree that the 'Improvement Sponsor' will delive the 'Opening Brief'	
3 WEEKS PRIOR TO VSE	**COMPLETE ✓**
Create 'Opening Brief' which normally is drawn straight from the 'Scoping Paper'	
Ask individuals in the areas affected to list what they believe are the 'Top 10 Hurts'	
Confirm the expected benefits from the VSE	

2 WEEKS PRIOR TO VSE	COMPLETE ✓
Finalise 'Opening Brief'	
Remind attendees about timings & venue	
2 WEEKS PRIOR TO VSE	**COMPLETE ✓**
Confirm all required data for event is available	
PRIOR TO THE VSE	
AGENDA	**DESCRIPTION**
• Opening Brief	Normally delivered by the 'Improvement Sponsor'
• Refresher Training	Refresher training for all staff involved in the process
• Current State	Identify how the process currently works using tools such as: • Process Analysis (Mapping) • Hand-Off Charts • String Diagrams • Data at a Glance • Questions to be Answered
• Daily Closing Brief	Delievered every evening (except the day before the final Closing Brief): • What has been achieved today • What questions need to be answered • What we will be doing tomorrow
• 'Blue Sky' State	Create a 'without boundaries' solution using: • Blue Sky Diagrams • Concept Capture Sheets • Opening Questioning

• Future State	Create a realistic plan of how the process will work in 6-12 months time: • Future State Map • Implementation Plan • Benefits Summary • Revised Layouts • Questions still to be answered
• Closing Brief	Delivered by the team, normally with the following agenda: • Welcome & overview of objectives • Review of the Current State • Review of the Blue Sky State • Review of the Future State • Review of the Implementation Plan & Benefits • Review of 'Lessons Learnt' • Questions

AFTER THE VSE	

1 WEEK AFTER VSE	COMPLETE ✓
Communicate the results of the VSE	
Confirm the 'Implementation Plan' and prepare for first events	
Ask team/s affected to identify how they will cope with the disruption of events	
Review all outstanding questions and obtain answers where possible	

2 WEEKS AFTER VSE	COMPLETE ✓
Undertake awareness briefings for all staff involved in first events	
Agree start-times and event duration for the first events	

Collect key process data, which often includes: • Activity Data (what do they do) • Volume (how often do each activity) • Touch Time (how much actual work is involved in doing each activity) • Lead Time (how long it takes from the start to the end)	
Get each team involved in first improvement events to identify their 'Top 10 Hurts'	
3 WEEKS AFTER VSE	**COMPLETE ✓**
Identify other preparatory work the team/s affected could do which could include: • Detailed Process Mapping • Hand-Off Charts • String Diagrams • Identification of 'Improvement Opportunities'	
Remind attendees about timings & venue/s	
4 WEEKS AFTER VSE	**COMPLETE ✓**
Undertake first improvement events	

Appendix 9

A Lean Parable for Practitioners everywhere

Once upon a time there lived a man named Clarence who had a pet frog named Eric. Clarence lived a modestly comfortable existence on what he earned working at the local supermarket, but he always dreamed of being rich.

"Eric!" Clarence exclaimed one day "We're going to be rich! I'm going to teach you how to fly!" Eric, of course, was terrified at the prospect. "I can't fly, you idiot! I'm a frog, not a canary!"

Clarence, disappointed at the initial reaction, told Eric "That negative attitude of yours could be a real problem. I'm sending you on a training course." So Eric went on a three day training course and learned all about problem solving, time management, and effective communication etc, but nothing about flying.

After the course was over, Clarence could barely control his excitement. He explained that the block of flats in which they lived had 15 floors, and each day Eric would jump out of a window starting with the first floor, eventually getting to the top floor. After each jump, Eric would analyse how well he flew, focus on the most effective flying techniques, and implement the improved process for the next flight. By the time they reached the top floor, Eric would surely be able to fly.

Eric pleaded for his life, but it fell on deaf ears. He just doesn't understand how important this is, thought Clarence, but I won't let nay sayers get in the way. With that, Clarence opened the window and threw Eric out. He landed with a thud.

Next day, poised for his second flying lesson, Eric again begged not to be thrown out of the window. With that Clarence opened his pocket guide to Managing More Effectively and showed Eric the part about how one must always expect resistance when implementing new programs. And with that, he threw him out of the window. (THUD)

On the third day (at the third floor window), Eric tried a different ploy: stalling. He asked for a delay in the project until better weather would make flying conditions more favourable. But Clarence was ready for him. He produced a project time line and pointed to the third milestone and asked "You don't want to miss the deadline, do you?"

From his training Eric knew that not jumping today would mean that he would have to jump TWICE tomorrow and with a sigh like a gentle wind he quietly said "OK. Let's go." (THUD)

Now this is not to say that Eric wasn't trying his best. On the fifth day he flapped his feet madly in a vain attempt to fly. THUD. On the sixth day he tied a small red cape around his neck and tried to think like Superman. But try as he may, he couldn't fly.

By the seventh day, Eric, accepting his fate, no longer begged for mercy. He looked pointedly at Clarence and said "You know you're killing me, don't you?"

Clarence pointed out that Eric's performance so far had been less than exemplary failing to meet any of the milestone goals he had set for him.

With that, Eric said quietly "Shut up and open the window." And he leaped out, taking careful aim on the large jagged rock by the corner of the building.

So Eric went to the great lily pad in the sky.

Clarence was extremely upset, as his project had failed to meet a single goal that he set out to accomplish.

Eric had not only failed to fly, he didn't even learn to steer his flight as he fell like a sack of cement ... nor did he improve when Clarence told him to fall smarter, not harder.

The only thing left for Clarence to do was to analyse the process and try to determine where it had gone wrong.

After much thought, Clarence smiled and said "Next time ... I'm getting a smarter frog!"

Lesson of this parable

Not all roadblocks and concerns that people raise during Lean Events are diversionary - some of them genuinely need to be addressed!

Printed in the United Kingdom
by Lightning Source UK Ltd.
131280UK00001B/76-342/P